DYLAN VAN DEN BERG is a Palawa writer and dramaturg. He has held residencies at Sydney Theatre Company through the Emerging Writers Group, at Griffin Theatre Company through the Studio Artist program, and was a participant in ILBIJERRI's BlackWrights program. His plays include *Whitefella Yella Tree* (Griffin Theatre Company), *Milk* (The Street Theatre), *Ngadjung* (Belco Arts), *The Camel* (Motley Bauhaus/FlickFlickCity), *All that Glitters is Not Mould* (NIDA), *The Chosen Vessel* (Early Phase: The Street Theatre) and *The Flood* (National Theatre of Parramatta). He is a two-time recipient of the Nick Enright Prize for Playwriting at the NSW Premier's Literary Awards, one time winner of the VIC Premier's Award for Drama, and was shortlisted for the UK's Bruntwood International Award for Playwriting. He studied theatre at the ANU and the State University of New York.

WHITEFELLA YELLA TREE

DYLAN VAN DEN BERG

CURRENCY PRESS
The performing arts publisher

CURRENCY PLAYS

First published in 2022
by Currency Press
Gadigal Land, Suite 310, 46–56 Kippax Street, Surry Hills, NSW 2010, Australia
enquiries@currency.com.au
www.currency.com.au

in association with Griffin Theatre.

This revised edition first published in 2023.

Typeset by Brighton Gray for Currency Press.
Cover features Callan Purcell and Guy Simon; photo by Brett Boardman.
Cover design by Emma Bennetts for Currency Press.

Currency Press acknowledges the Traditional Owners of the Country on which we live and work. We pay our respects to all Aboriginal and Torres Strait Islander Elders, past and present.

A catalogue record for this book is available from the National Library of Australia

Contents

Introduction

Have you ever been in love?

Like heedlessly in love, like you could run at break-neck speed, like your heart could beat out of your chest, like you would do anything for a moment to be prolonged, like you want to tell each and every soul about the person that makes you warm?

This is a play that is steeped in love and the feelings of being in love. It is also a story on the impact colonisation has on love.

In the early 1800s, two young fellas, Neddy, a warrior from the Mountain Mob and Ty, a storyteller from the River Mob, meet under the Yella Tree at every full moon—to share intel about the recently arrived invaders and pass it back to their communities.

The characters of Neddy and Ty are like star-crossed lovers of the nineteenth-century Australian bush but in Dylan Van Den Berg's hands, this story does not need to race to end in tragedy or without poetic justice, and it might not. I implore you to pay special attention to the direction the story takes and the path it leaves in Dylan's craft. Like the shape a snake makes as it slivers through Country, it is made by water, wind, sun and fire.

What does a story hold?

The relationship is the frame in which we understand the story.

This story is directive to a lack of queer Blak characters in the 'canon' of plays, books, and film, and by extension, a lack of queer Blak love stories, especially those who brave joy, pleasure and growth.

These two beautiful youngfellas on the cusp of everything: manhood, awakening, grief, it is like we know them, it is like we feel them, it is like we listen to their heartbeats.

It also a story that connects to a broader movement of Blak contemporary theatre that is subverting Western expectations and bringing the power of Aboriginal and Torres Strait Islander storytelling to new audiences.

It is also a love story that just happens to be queer.

When Neddy and Ty tell their loved ones, a sister, and an Aunty, about their budding love interest, the response is purely supportive, not one of surprise or conflict. This normalises the relationship. With teenage giddiness and the security of acceptance from mob, Ty and Neddy both declare, 'You'll be the first to meet him.'

I have experienced my own queer Black love, and it is the series of infinite time capsules and activation of truth bombs that Neddy and Ty experience in their relationship. The love between queer Blak people is woven in the complexities of multi-time. For my lover and I, our Country and mobs couldn't be further apart but we shared in a history of connection and culture, then brutalisation and fracturing, and reconnection and hope under the weight of intergenerational trauma and traumatic grief. My east coast lingo merged with her west coast lingo, and slowly we navigated a path of pleasure and connection in an urbanised place, the Country on Country, the distances and differences in space and time, the family and kin, and what she loved became what I loved and what I loved became what she loved. All this is to say that when a Blak person loves another Blak person, and they are queer, it is beautiful.

The conversations between the two queer young men are tender. In the blend of historical setting with contemporary speech and gestures, the world is open and familiar. I appreciated the cheeky Blak humour in their banter that welcomes you from the first page.

Dylan's script is one of the most beautiful scripts you'll read. It's lean, compelling and full of moments that I found deeply tense and moving. It is very easy to see why the judges awarded this work the Nick Enright Prize for Playwriting at the 2023 NSW Premiers' Literary Awards, Dylan's second Nick Enright Prize, after winning the first one for his previous work, *Milk*.

In their Nick Enright Award citation for *Whitefella Yella Tree*, the judges remarked: 'There are few plays in the Australian repertoire that weave sweetness and savagery, and the personal and the political, as finely as this. This is a devastating, but delicate play, and one that deserves to be produced many times.'

Now to retell some biographical details on Dylan Van Den Berg. He is a Canberra writer. His mob are Palawa. He is an exciting young voice in Australian theatre. I can't wait to see what he does next.

What can we say about the Yella Tree, or lemon tree—the image that holds the play together? Nobody knows where this Yella Tree has come from, but Ty and Neddy have their theories. The tree is an intruding figure on Country, it doesn't belong. It is growing. It is changing. Bearing fruit. The Yella Tree is witness to everything.

Ty and Neddy meet at the lemon tree to discuss the happenings and movements of the whitefellas and pass on important information that's crucial to survival. They grow older and wiser.

Each time the young men meet another stage of colonisation has begun. The River Mobs and the Mountain Mobs watch the whitefellas put their marks on country—watching, waiting, anticipating, strategising.

One meeting, a hat draped on the branches of the tree indicates the whitefellas have already encroached on their meeting space and come up their way.

The playwright cleverly refuses to overtly show the white invaders—their faces, their smells, their smiles, their violence—on page and stage. He only shows the impact that these people, and their supremacist acts, have on people and Country. Where queerphobia and colonisation merge, and choke our mob.

Love has, forcefully, been a subject of settler poets and lyricists. From Dorothea Mackellar's 'I love a sunburned country, a land of sweeping plains, of rugged mountain ranges...', to 'My Country' or the bush ballads of Henry Lawson. Dylan Van Den Berg includes whitefella song; 'Oh, No, We Never Mention Her' by Thomas Haynes Bayly in the script. When Neddy sings this love tune by the river, draped in settler clothing, we see a collision of fate, a glimpse of what may be to come.

I am in favour of works that lean into poetry, and the poetics of the work are startling.

Every moment feels heightened through language.

When I first received the script to read I was floored by it. I read the script again several times as if to soak in its brilliance and strip back the magic that was flowing from the alchemy of words. Like paperbark, the script is softly textured but has a solid interior. Where many lifeforms live.

The emotional power these men have over each other is both mental and physical; and this dynamic love story between young men during invasion is a welcome addition to writing about Blak masculinity.

The challenges Ty and Neddy face are many and they are both individual and shared. The roles they play in their community indicate responsibilities and knowledge systems that are earned through trust and demonstration of ability.

There's more than just romantic love here. Like Neddy's strong desperate protective love for his sister, which drives him to join the whitefella world in search of information after she is captured. And both of the men's love for their mobs which complements their love for each other.

They meet at every full moon and eventually their bodies meet too. Their friendly teasing banter soon makes way for closeness, physical closeness, which comes at a risk with an encroaching epidemic—smallpox—this new foreign disease that is raging against the bodies of those who belong to Country and are especially vulnerable.

As the whitefella ways start to intrude on the young men, the shame starts to creep in, something that was not there before. And the old stories start to fade and distort and disappear and Ty tries to remember the stories of the river essential to keeping him alive.

This is contested space—both in Country and in story.

There are lessons here: love is not danger. Love is not destructive. Love knows no boundaries or borders.

Whitefella Yella Tree is about responsibility, and sacrifice and pride. This is a work that is full of life. This work has gifts for all of us, though I grow especially happy thinking about its potential reach to a young audience.

We need more stories like this. Our hearts have been aching for too long, and silently for stories like this.

Thank you, Dylan, for writing this story for us.

Ellen van Neerven

Mununjali mob

Written on Jagera and Turrbal Land, 2023

Whitefella Yella Tree was first produced by Griffin Theatre Company at the SBW Stables Theatre, Darlinghurst, Gadigal Country, on 19 August 2022 with the following cast:

TY	Callan Purcell
NEDDY	Guy Simon

Co-Directors, Declan Greene and Amy Sole
Designer, Mason Browne
Lighting Designer, Kelsey Lee
Composer and Sound Designer, Steve Toulmin
Dramaturg, Andrea James
Stage Manager, Isabella Kerdijk

CHARACTERS

NEDDY. A young Aboriginal man. Ages from a teenager to a young man. Warrior.

TY. A young Aboriginal man. Ages from a teenager to a young man. Storyteller.

SETTING/TIME

Sometime during the early period of colonisation.

A place somewhere between a mountain and a river.

NOTES

Nearly everything happens in the same place – under a lemon tree.

It gets bigger as the play goes on.

Even though we're in the early 1800s, the boys still look and sound like they're from 'now'.

1.

A lemon tree.

Thorny, knotted branches stretching out and up.

Greeny-yellow leaves.

Tiny white blossoms with yellow pistils.

(That's what the centre of a blossom is called.)

There's a bit of scrub.

Maybe we can hear the river.

TY *sits under the tree, impatient.*

Suddenly—

Some movement.

NEDDY *darts between bushes.*

Rolling, leaping, tiptoeing.

Trying to move, unnoticed, towards the lemon tree.

He settles in a bush nearby, watching.

Some silence.

TY: You can come out.

> NEDDY *doesn't move.*

I'm not dumb.
> I know you're there.

> *Silence.*

Look, you're late enough already.
> Really late.

> TY *picks up a rock.*

> *He lobs it into the bushes.*

> *It lands on* NEDDY.

NEDDY: Oi! What the—

TY: Sooner you get your arse out here, sooner I can leave.

NEDDY: Chuckin' rocks like a—a—a—

TY: What?

NEDDY: Say sorry.

TY: For what?

NEDDY: For chuckin' the rock.

TY: Sorry?

 Pfft.

 Wish I found a bigger one. Could've knocked you out cold and left you here for the birds.

 Where've you been?

NEDDY: Been sneakin', haven't I?

 NEDDY *emerges from the bushes.*

 But then—

Hang on hang on—

 NEDDY *retreats again.*

What's your code name?

TY: Seriously?

NEDDY: Told ya last time—

 Arrive at the tree—

TY: Got it.

NEDDY: Announce yourself—but with ya code name.

 Then—

TY: Shut up, Neddy—

NEDDY: Oi! No real names around here!

TY: Sorry Neddy.

 Whoopsie.

 TY *covers his mouth with his hands.*

NEDDY: You better pull ya head in before I … get up and—

 Biff ya nose.

TY: Scary.

NEDDY: Just give me ya code name!

TY: Are you fifteen, or five?

NEDDY: Code name—

TY: I don't remember.

NEDDY: Don't remember? Pretty important.

TY: What's yours?

NEDDY: Feisty Fish.

TY: Because you're … tough and *slippery*?

NEDDY: Yeah.

　　　No.

　　　'Feisty' as in, like, you know—

TY: I don't.

NEDDY: And 'fish' as in—

TY: Cold blooded?

NEDDY: No—? Fish as in—

TY: You don't have eyelids?

NEDDY: Fish as in *quick*.

　　　Your turn now—I ain't comin' out for just anyone.

TY: You know who I am—

NEDDY: Your code name.

　　　Starts with 'S'.

　　　Pause.

TY: Ssssss …

　　　NEDDY *nods encouragingly.*

　'Slinky' … ?

NEDDY: Nah.

TY: 'Sneaky' … ?

NEDDY: No.

TY: Saucy—

NEDDY: *No*—

TY: Stylish—

NEDDY: No—

TY: Super fuckin' … Slick.

NEDDY: No!

TY: I don't know—

NEDDY: It's 'Silent'!

　　　Silent Moth.

　　　Pause.

TY: Yeah. I'm gonna pick something else.

NEDDY: You can't just *change* ya code name—

TY: Don't remember coming to any kind of *agreement*—

NEDDY: You got somethin' better?

> *Pause.*

TY: I'll stick with the moth.

NEDDY: Good.

> I reckon you are who you say you are.
>
> My name's Neddy! Code name Feisty Fish! I'm *Mountain* Mob! Here to pass on information about the whitefellas!
>
> > NEDDY *makes a strange movement.*
> >
> > *Kind of like when someone does a 'dab'.*
> >
> > *The kind of move that says—*
> >
> > *'There, I said it—whatchagonna do?'*

TY: My name's Ty.

> Code name: Silent Moth.
>
> River Mob.
>
> Now, can we just get this done?
>
> Don't fancy walking back in the dark.
>
> *Pause.*

NEDDY: Okay.

TY: Okay.

> Feel free.
>
> To exchange.

NEDDY: I ain't goin' first.

> *Pause.*

TY: Well.

> Last time there were only a few of them. Now they've like doubled. Cleared a spot by the river—right at the neck that goes into the ocean. The ground'll be too salty for them to plant anything, but that doesn't seem to be stopping them. They take up space—with their bodies and piles of shit—but also their … voices? Like, the air gets filled up with their *sound*—it gets thick with grunting and snorting and bellowing and it's almost like you could rest your head on it—
>
> Like, the air.
>
> You know?
>
> *Pause.*

NEDDY: Yeah nah.

TY: Well—

Anyway.

We counted at least six different words they used, over and over.

We think one means 'water'.

And another one probably means 'fuck'.

They said that the most.

You?

NEDDY: We're high up, so we get the best view of what they're doin'.

TY: Sure.

NEDDY: Little white specks trippin' over rocks and trying to build shelter.

Saw one take a dump on an ant nest.

Pause.

Exchange over.

TY: Is that all?

NEDDY: Yep.

TY: Where are they located? How many are there? Have they moved any closer? What weapons do they have?

You got anything?

NEDDY: Nah.

Just the ant nest thing.

TY: I gave you words—*actual* words and specific locations—

NEDDY: You gave me a shit poem, basically.

How am I gonna take that back to the Elders?

'Oh, Uncle—sorry, nothing much to report, but I *do* have this description of the air and how *thick* it becomes when a whitefella does a burp.'

TY: And I'm supposed to go back and say—

'Oh, Aunty—you know how we were *just* saying the ants have been smelling a bit like poo lately? Turns out whitefellas are shitting at the source!'

NEDDY: You're welcome.

Pause.

TY: Exchange over.

TY *reaches up and picks a blossom from the tree.*

He looks at it closely.

NEDDY: That wasn't here last time.

TY: That's how trees work. Dickhead.

NEDDY: You don't know all the trees, so maybe stop being such a stuck-up prick.

TY: Pricks can grow—just like trees. You're learning.

NEDDY: Shut-up, dipstick.

TY: Shut-up, shit-for-brains.

NEDDY: Butterfly dick.

TY: Wet log.

NEDDY: Wombat … licker.

> TY *and* NEDDY *try to hide their amusement.*

> TY *smells the blossom.*

How is it?

> TY *holds out the blossom.* NEDDY *sniffs it.*

Kind of nice.

TY: Not bad.

> *Pause.*

NEDDY: Do you mind if I—

> Like, can I have that?

TY: You want it?

NEDDY: Yeah.

> For my sister.

> She loves flowers and the way they smell and she dries 'em out in the sun till they're crunchy and she makes these, like, little … groups? Like, arrangements. And they're so fucking pretty—

> *Pause.*

> NEDDY*'s voice goes a bit deeper.*

Promised I'd take her somethin' back.

> You know what sisters are like.

TY: I don't.

> Hope she likes it.

> TY *gives* NEDDY *the flower.*

NEDDY: So.

See ya back here?

TY: Next moon.

They both linger. TY notices the sun sinking away. It will be dark soon.

Why'd you have to be so late?

Can't head back now.

NEDDY: I've never lost a race against the sun.

NEDDY *goes to leave.*

TY *doesn't move.*

You scared?

TY: What? Not scared. Never been *scared*. Just … getting my bearings.

NEDDY: Cool.

TY: Actually—

You probably should stay.

NEDDY: Why?

TY: Because—

Because there's some information I need to share.

It's very … secret.

And when you've got information that's … secret—you can't be too careful.

NEDDY: Just tell me what it is?

TY: No!

NEDDY: No?

TY: Someone could be …

TY *motions to his ear.*

[*Whispering*] Listening …

NEDDY: Out here?

[*Whispering*] Whitefellas?

TY *nods solemnly.*

TY: [*whispering*] They've got these special things. Like, machines. Long, long sticks. With, like, ears strapped to the end. And they can sit far, far away, holding one end of the stick, pushing the ears deeper deeper deeper into the bush and listening to whoever is out there.

Pause.

NEDDY: Ears on a stick.
TY: Yep.

Pause.

NEDDY: You're full of shit.
TY: No—it's actually true—
NEDDY: It's getting dark—
TY: I heard about it from—
NEDDY: If I don't head off—
TY: My nan—
NEDDY: I won't make it.

Pause.

I better get goin'.
TY: Alright alright alright.
        Can you just—
        Like—
        You know—
        If you just—
        Don't go—
        If you just—
        Stay—
        Because I have a—
        Sore … spot.
        An injury.
        Ouchie.

TY feigns an injury.

He touches his elbow and then his knee, but settles on his toe as the point of pain.

Can you take a look?
NEDDY: Seriously?
TY: Please.

TY puts his foot up against the lemon tree.

NEDDY reluctantly checks TY's toe.

NEDDY: Looks fine.

TY: Doesn't feel fine.

You sure?

NEDDY: Pretty sure.

Pause.

Alright—I'm gonna—

TY: You hungry?

NEDDY: Not really.

TY: Have some of this. Don't wanna carry it all the way back. Especially not now that I'm injured.

TY *pulls some food out of his bag.*

NEDDY: Thanks.

NEDDY *eats awkwardly while* TY *watches him.*

TY *yawns loudly.*

TY: We should probably just … stay?

Pause.

NEDDY *makes a decision to stay.*

NEDDY: Okay.

TY: Okay!

An awkward silence.

TY *and* NEDDY *look at each other.*

It's tense and exciting and strange.

Like something could happen.

NEDDY *takes a step towards* TY.

TY *quickly busies himself looking for a spot to sleep.*

Umm—

Yep!

Sleepy time!

NEDDY: Not dark yet.

TY: Close your eyes, then.

NEDDY: I'm not tired.

Pause.

TY: I'll sleep over here.

NEDDY: Oh? There?

TY: Yes?

> I mean—
>
> Yes.
>
> Why wouldn't I? Is there something wrong with sleeping here?

NEDDY: No no no no. It's just. Yeah.

> *I* wouldn't wanna sleep there.

> TY *leaps up.*

TY: Why? What? What is it?

NEDDY: Well.

> Wind comin' in from that way—

> NEDDY *points.*

Big gust could come through and snap—

> Branch comes down and strikes ya in the heart.

> NEDDY *laughs and acts out being stabbed in the heart by a branch.*

So—

> Glad *you're* gonna be there.

TY: I didn't mean exactly there—just in that direction.

> I'll sleep here.

NEDDY: There?

> Oh, boy.
>
> You ever heard of the … snappers?

TY: Shut up. No such thing.

NEDDY: Crawl up out of the dirt at night—thin like worms with teeth like tiny dingos—and they snap up ya brains.

> It's why they're called snappers—
>
> 'Cause they eat ya brains.

TY: I guess you're safe then.

NEDDY: Eh?

TY: From the snappers.

NEDDY: No-one's safe from the snappers.

> Not if you sleep right on top of a nest. Like you.

TY: But you said they eat brains.

NEDDY: Yeah. They do.

TY: So you've got nothing to worry about.

> *Pause.*

NEDDY: Oh.
> Oh.
> Yeah.
> Ha.
> Think you're smart, don't ya?

> *Pause.*

TY: Yeah. Sure.
> That's what everyone says.

NEDDY: Must be nice.

> *Pause.*

TY: Not when it's your job.
> I have to know everything—
> And if I don't know it—
> I have to ask the question.
> Imagine looking at everything, and either knowing about it, or knowing that you have to know about it, eventually.

NEDDY: Like what?

TY: Like—
> The clouds.
> They're made of this … smoke. You can see it, taste it, maybe even feel it—like, a bit of a chill on your arms and your neck. But you can't grab hold of it.
> Telling a lie is like breathing out a cloud. Looks real, but if someone tries to grab hold of it—there'll be nothing there.
> It's why frogs poke their tongues out—
> Well, this one frog—
> Sits up on a mountain, checking the misty air around him for lies, day after day.
> That's the kind of thing I'm learning from the Elders.

> *Pause.*

NEDDY: I wouldn't lie to a frog.

TY: What?

NEDDY *is deep in thought for a moment.*

NEDDY: You know a fair bit.

> TY *shrugs.*

TY: If I had a choice, I'd be a warrior instead.
Ka-pow!!

> TY *does a karate chop. It's a bit shit.*

NEDDY: I think ya Elders made the right choice.

TY: What's that supposed to mean?

NEDDY: Nothin'.

TY: I'm working on the muscles.

NEDDY: … 'the muscles'?

> TY *drops down and does a few push-ups.*

> *He speaks in between each one.*

TY: I do—
This—
Every—
Day—

> NEDDY *places his foot on* TY*'s back, making it harder for him.*

Hey—
I'm not ready for—
Extra weight—
Yet—

> NEDDY *picks* TY *up.*

> *Shows off his strength for a bit.*

Put me down put me down put me down put me DOWN—

> NEDDY *places* TY *under the tree.*

> *Pause.*

NEDDY: Now, using ya brain for a moment—no disrespect to 'the muscles'—
What do you reckon about this tree?

TY: It's been here for a while—

NEDDY: No-one knows, do they?

Look at it. Green-yellow-pissy-coloured leaves.

Some folks say it came outta the ground—outta nowhere.

Like, the earth just opened up and out came this branch and it grew and grew and grew right in front of them.

TY: You believe that?

NEDDY: Nah. It's bullshit.

I got my own theory.

TY: Based on what?

NEDDY *shrugs*.

NEDDY: Puttin' two and two together.

Sometimes you just know stuff, you know?

So.

I reckon it goes like this.

Years and years ago, a whitefella fell out of the sky.

TY: Here we go.

NEDDY: Knocked him about a bit, didn't it?

There was all this stuff around him—

Rocks bigger than roos, bird nests hangin' in trees, wallabies stickin' their teeth out—

But after the fall, he didn't just see rocks and nests and wallabies.

Somethin' happened in his brain.

To him, the rocks looked like … naked women—

TY: Sorry, what?

NEDDY: And the nests looked like tits and the wallabies looked like buff fellas with no clothes.

And the whitefella got a bit, like, excited, you know, seein' all these sexy rocks and wallabies—

TY: Which he thought were people—

NEDDY: Gave him a boner. Not a big one—

More like a twig—

Could barely find it in his pubes.

Rubbed it between his pinky and his thumb like he tryin' to start a tiny fire for a couple of ants.

NEDDY *pretends to jerk off a tiny appendage.*

And he rubbed and rubbed and rubbed and—

NEDDY *pretends to climax.*

Splodged right here on the ground.
    Then it grew—
    Up and up and up.

TY: What happened to the whitefella?

NEDDY: Whacked off so much he died.

TY: I reckon it's actually two lovers, bound together for disobeying a spirit.
    She was a beautiful woman—the spirit—and any man who saw her would, like, faint.
    But one day, two lovers came along, and they only had eyes for each other—
    And they didn't faint, because she had no power over them—
    So she turned them into trees.

NEDDY: That'll teach 'em.

TY: So here are the lovers, together, but not *together*.

    Pause.

NEDDY: My yarn's better.

TY: If you reckon.

NEDDY: I do.
    I call it the yella tree.

TY: Everyone calls it the yella tree.
    It's literally what our mobs have called it.

NEDDY: Yeah, but I had the idea first.

TY: Goodnight Neddy.

NEDDY: I actually did.

TY: Goodnight Neddy.

NEDDY: I did!

TY: Go the fuck to sleep.

    The sun sets.

    The boys lay in the dark.

(A)

The yella tree grows.
The branches twist into the sky.
The roots disturb the earth.
The boys appear and re-appear.
They're growing up.
They play dumb games.
There's a moment when TY *finds himself looking at* NEDDY.
There's a moment when NEDDY *finds himself looking at* TY.
There's a moment where they catch each other looking.
There's a moment where they have an inexplicable wrestle, because why not.
There's a moment of danger.
A sound or a shadow or something.
The boys register it—but just for a moment.
A hat falls down from the tree.
It doesn't belong here.

2.

In whitefella time, a year or so later.
Late afternoon.
Lemons scattered across the ground.
TY *appears, looking up at the yella tree.*
He's grown up a bit.
He's slow dancing, almost like he's in a club and Mariah Carey's
'Touch my Body' is playing.

TY: What're you looking at, huh?
      You like what you see, huh?
      Can't blame you for looking.
      You're an ugly bastard.

But the sunset's got me all giddy.
Giving you the right amount of shadow.
Lighting up bits I've never seen before.
But just looking, alright?
Branches to yourself.
Twigs where I can see 'em.
Just watching—
Me—
The sun—
The light—
The—

NEDDY *suddenly appears.*

NEDDY: Woooooow.
TY: Fuck shit fuck!

Don't kill me please—

NEDDY *laughs.*

NEDDY: That. Was. Fucking. Great.
Silent Moth spreads his wings—

NEDDY *imitates* TY, *dancing and speaking to the tree.*

'Hey there, big fella.'
'Hope I'm not barkin' up the wrong tree.'
TY: Fuck you.
That was just—
NEDDY: I could actually die now.
I'm only sixteen, but I'd be fine with it.
TY: You broke protocol—
Your own fucking *rules*—
Not announcing yourself—
And just *watching*.
You—
Perve.
NEDDY: Guilty.

Pause.

Never thought of *dancin'* for the whitefellas.
But you know, shoot ya shot.

NEDDY *notices the lemons.*

What the fuck are these?

TY: From the tree.

NEDDY: Might take some back—

NEDDY *starts collecting lemons.*

Sis loves weird shit.
She can keep 'em near all her dead bugs.

NEDDY *notices the hat.*

Ty. Look.

Pause.

They've never come up this far.
Have they?

TY: Ummm—

NEDDY: Have they?

TY: Not that we've seen—

TY *looks around.*

Maybe it just landed here?
Dropped by a bird or blew in the wind.

NEDDY: I dunno.

TY: They were probably just lost.

NEDDY: Maybe.

TY *approaches the hat.*

Ty, don't touch it!
You don't know—

TY: It's fine.

It's just a—

TY *screams and throws the hat towards* NEDDY.

NEDDY *screams and drops his armful of lemons.*

NEDDY: GET IT OFF GET IT OFF GET IT OFF GET IT OFF!
What the—

TY *thinks this is hysterical.*

Should leave the jokes to someone who's actually *funny.*

TY: Uh-huh.

>NEDDY *sulks.*

>TY *picks up the hat.*

>*He shakes it back into shape.*

>*He dusts off some of the dirt.*

>*He puts it on* NEDDY*'s head.*

Cute.

Suits you.

Except for your skin—and your face—and your voice—and your hair—you could pass as a whitefella.

NEDDY: Ya reckon?

TY: Totally.

>TY *picks up a lemon.*

Wanna try one?

NEDDY: Ewww. No.

TY: Come on.

Just bite straight into it.

NEDDY: Ya reckon?

>NEDDY *taps the lemon against the tree.*

TY: Yeah, just rip into it with your teeth.

NEDDY: You go first.

TY: Can't *both* lose our teeth, can we?

NEDDY: Nah. This is fucked.

TY: Come on.

NEDDY: Pretty dumb just to eat somethin'—

TY: Pretty dumb not to try—

NEDDY: Don't even know what it is—

TY: Thought you knew all about the yella tree—

NEDDY: Heard about it—

Different to *knowin'* about it—

TY: Sometimes you just need to be *fearless*—

Have no fear.

Just do it.

>*Pause.*

NEDDY: I'm not scared—
>It's just—
>Arm wrestle.

TY: What?

NEDDY: Arm wrestle. Let's do one.

TY: Why—?

NEDDY: Whoever loses eats it.

TY: Whoever loses?

NEDDY: Yep.

>*Pause.*

TY: You'll win.

NEDDY: Maybe.

TY: I barely have arms.

NEDDY: What about a race then?
>To the top of the tree.
>I've got muscles, right?

>NEDDY *flexes.*

But you're small.
>And you move like a lizard.
>Like, a nice one.
>A pretty one.

TY: Alright.

NEDDY: Whoever grabs that one—

>NEDDY *points to a lemon at the top of the tree.*

Is the winner.

TY: Good luck.

NEDDY: Keep it for yourself.

>NEDDY *and* TY *arrange themselves at the base of the tree.*

Ready?
>One—
>Two—
>Three—
>Boom!

>NEDDY *and* TY *scale the tree.*

TY *approaches it slowly, considering the best path to the top.*

NEDDY *approaches it like a wombat doing silks.*

And he's quick, aye—
　　Faster than a dingo—
　　Stronger than a—
　　Just strong—
　　And he slinks up the tree like a very *very* quick koala—
TY: Quiet please—
NEDDY: His challenger is jealous—
　　But he won't let that stop him—
　　'Cause—

TY *reaches the top just before* NEDDY.

TY/NEDDY: I win!
TY: I got it first.
NEDDY: Technically you didn't because—
TY: I touched the fucking lemon—
NEDDY: I had the sun in my eyes—
TY: Yeah right—
NEDDY: Too close to call—
TY: Pfft—
NEDDY: It was!

　　Pause.

TY: Alright.
NEDDY: I guess it's a tie. Ty.
TY: Yeah. A tie.

TY *and* NEDDY *drop to the ground.*

TY *finds a rock.*

He smashes the lemon in half.

TY: Here.
　　If we *both* won, we also both kind of lost.
NEDDY: Alright.
　　If I die—
TY: Don't think about it—
　　Here we go!

NEDDY *and* TY *cheers with their lemon segments.*

They taste it.

Their faces scrunch and twist.

But—

They want to put on a brave face for one another.

TY: Yeah.
It's ummm—
NEDDY: Not too bad.
TY: Yep.
NEDDY: Might have some more.
TY: Go for it.

NEDDY *takes another bite.*

They look at each other with their contorted faces.

Pause.

NEDDY: Fuck that shit.
TY: It's shit.
NEDDY: Do you reckon we're dead?
My mouth feels dead.

NEDDY *throws the lemon into the distance.*

TY *and* NEDDY *look at each other.*

They laugh.

They stop.

They move closer.

They could kiss.

But—

TY *spits out some lemon.*

The moment's over.

TY: Sun'll be gone soon, so we should … do the exchange.
NEDDY: Oh. Yeah.

NEDDY *starts piffing more lemons into the bush.*

TY *joins in.*

As they piff, they exchange information.

They caught us killing sheep.

Fluffy bastards eatin' everything green as far as you could see, so we knocked a couple off.

Swear they give more fucks about those fat little clouds than they do people.

Before that, and it's pretty chill but, like, we traded with 'em.

TY: What?

NEDDY: The whitefellas.

TY: Fuuuuuck.

How did that even—

Like—

What the—

NEDDY: It was fine, you know?

TY: Did you meet them?

NEDDY: Well, no—

Only the Elders.

But, like, I could see the whole thing from a tree.

So I was *basically* there.

They gave us stuff. Like, whitefella stuff.

Food.

A mirror. So you can see your own face whenever you want.

TY: Got a river for that.

NEDDY: A clip for my sister's hair.

Shaped like a flower, 'cause she—

TY: Loves flowers.

NEDDY: Yeah.

TY: And they just left?

NEDDY: We thought that. Thought they'd piss off somewhere else.

But they brought up all their sheep. And they started stuffin' their faces and stompin' on everything.

And—

And they chose me to kill 'em.

Uncle said I was ready, that I was strong enough and quick enough and *smart* enough.

And it felt … good, you know?

To *do*. Instead of to watch or wait or whatever.

Pause.

TY: That's … brave.

Sounds like you were ready.

NEDDY: You reckon?

TY: Yeah.

NEDDY: Well, now they're running out of sheep and they're pretty pissed about it, so we gotta be careful.

TY: They've started to cut down trees. And they've been putting plants in the ground. Plants we've never seen before.

First I thought they must be, like, little yella trees?

Anyway, when it's dark, our mob pull 'em back out again. Pull them out, leave them next to the hole. Looks like a bunch of tiny green skeletons.

And get this—

Every morning, they stomp their feet and shake their fists at the sky—like the clouds pulled 'em out or something.

NEDDY: You get to do it?

TY: Nah.

I'm not—

Ready.

Too much to learn.

Every day, a new story or ceremony or whatever.

Elders are worried, I think.

Pause.

There's so much to know about the river, you know?

Like—

Ummmm—

How it's like a caterpillar.

Moves slowly.

When the rain comes, the caterpillar moves.

Changes shape.

And someone's gotta know how to follow it if—

You know.

NEDDY: I know.

TY: Anyway.

Exchange over.

Pause.

NEDDY: I reckon that's pretty brave, too.

TY: Maybe.

> TY *picks up the hat.*
>
> *He throws it away.*

NEDDY: Better let you get back to ya tree dancin'.

> *They look at each other.*
>
> *They don't want to leave.*

See ya.

TY: Bye.

NEDDY: Bye.

> *Pause.*

TY: See you at—

NEDDY: Next moon.

TY: Next moon.

TY/NEDDY: Well—

NEDDY: I better—

TY/NEDDY: Go.

> *Pause.*

NEDDY: I'm gonna go—

TY: That way—

> TY *points.*

NEDDY: No—

TY: Oh.

NEDDY: That's the way to *your* mob.

TY: Ah.

NEDDY: I'm gonna go—

TY: Silly me—

NEDDY: Nah—

TY: Well—

NEDDY: It's dark—

TY: It *is* dark—

NEDDY: Hard to know which way is—

TY/NEDDY: Which.

Pause.

NEDDY: Night, Ty.

TY: Night Neddy.

Night Neddy.

Ha.

Try saying that—

Lots of times.

Night Neddy night Neddy night Neddy night Neddy.

Pause.

NEDDY: Pretty tricky, eh.

Pause.

TY/NEDDY: Bye.

TY *and* NEDDY *leave.*

Smiling and puffed up with teenage giddiness.

(B)

TY *and* NEDDY *are in different spaces.*

TY *speaks to his aunty.*

NEDDY *speaks to his sister.*

TY: Aunty—he looks like something carved out of rock—

NEDDY: Sis—he's like a splash of water, right on your face—

TY: He says dumb things literally constantly—

NEDDY: He knows stuff. Like *knows* it, you know?

And he listens—

TY: And I can't—

NEDDY: I can't stop … thinking.

TY: Him.

NEDDY: About him.

TY: Everything I look at reminds me of him.

I see a stone and I think of his eyes.

I see a fire and I think of his warm breath, up close.

I see a frog—and I think of his, like, *bounce.*

Is that normal, Aunty?

NEDDY: You'll feel it one day, Sis.

Your blood'll get hot and you'll feel woozy in your stomach—'cept you won't throw up everywhere.

It's its own thing.

TY/NEDDY: And he said I'm brave.

TY: Me.

NEDDY: Me.

TY/NEDDY: I'm fucked.

TY: We haven't exactly—

NEDDY: We haven't kissed.

TY: Or held hands.

NEDDY: Or touched, even.

TY/NEDDY: But I want to.

NEDDY: Fuck I want to.

TY: Aunty, I don't need to know that.

NEDDY: Sis, you're waaaaay to young to know that.

I think I'd just like to hold him and touch his hair and let him feel my arms 'cause he probably wants to do that.

TY: I want to feel his arms. Both of them.

NEDDY: Then I'll lay him down on the grass or the dirt or whatever, and we won't feel the rocks digging into our backs.

TY: And Aunty?

NEDDY: And Sis?

TY/NEDDY: You'll be the first to meet him.

(C)

Gunshots.

Chaos.

We see NEDDY *running, searching, scared.*

Sound of horses thundering along the ground.

Distant yelling.

NEDDY *hides.*

He doesn't know what to do.

3.

Late afternoon.

NEDDY *leans against the yella tree.*

He's troubled.

He's building something. Maybe out of sticks and rocks. Or out of whitefella materials he's found. Or both.

TY *appears.*

TY: Sorry sorry sorry sorry—
      Had to come a different way and I tried to be quick—
      Got legs like two dead snakes.

      TY *notices* NEDDY*'s machine.*

  What's that?

      NEDDY *shrugs.*

  You okay?

      NEDDY *shrugs.*

  You gonna talk?
      Neddy?

NEDDY: Whitefellas found us again.

TY: What?

NEDDY: But I've got a plan—

TY: Wait—

NEDDY: It'll be—

TY: Are you hurt?

NEDDY: No—

TY: You got away—

NEDDY: Quicker than them, ain't I?
      Smashed their heads in.
      They didn't know what was comin'.

TY: You were fighting?

NEDDY: Took on three—
      No—
      Four—

At once.
Maybe even five.
Distracted me so I didn't see 'em take—

Pause.

TY: Neddy.
What happened?
NEDDY: They took a whole heap of us.
Rounded 'em up.
And they—
They—
Took my sister, too.
Grabbed her by the hair.

Pause.

Exchange over.

TY doesn't know what to say.

He sits down next to NEDDY.

NEDDY turns his attention back to building his contraption.

Gonna make a … a … machine.
To get her back.
Got it all … planned.
Gonna distract 'em.
Gonna blow 'em up.
Like lightning to a dead tree.
And I'll bring her back home.

TY looks at the sticks and rocks and bits and pieces.

TY: How does it work?

NEDDY picks up a stick and draws a diagram in the dirt for TY.

NEDDY: I'm gonna make a frame first—something to hold it all together.
Maybe outta these sticks, or with reeds from the river … or somethin' else.
And then inside … I gotta get these rocks to stay in place.
Like, they're all bound together really tight and they look like *one* rock.
But when I pull down on this … this … stick—

The rocks will explode—pull apart—they'll fly everywhere in every direction and smash 'em in the face. Won't kill 'em, I don't reckon. But hurt 'em enough so I can sneak in and … and …

TY: Get your sister.

Pause.

NEDDY: Anyway, still workin' on it.

The Old People won't let me go—they said I gotta stay.

But when I show 'em this—they'll let me.

That's what I reckon.

TY: Sounds like you got it figured out.

NEDDY: Yeah?

TY: Yep.

Pause.

You know how you told that bullshit story about the yella tree?

NEDDY: Not bullshit.

But yeah.

TY: Well, it *is*.

Because I heard the *real* story.

NEDDY: When?

TY: This morning.

NEDDY: Don't have time for stories.

TY: There was a warrior.

With a duty to protect something very special.

He whispered to everything around him—

The ground. The waterways. The sky.

And it whispered back.

They understood each other.

But one day, the warrior faltered.

He forgot to talk to the dirt and the blue up over his head.

He forgot to gently call to the river.

And he was punished.

Walking through a swamp one day, his feet got stuck in the mud.

He was stuck for days and getting hungry and tired and his muscles started to shrink away.

The spirits said—

'You will suffer—'

'We will keep you here till there's nothing left but your bones and your ballsack!'
And they did.

TY *points to the lemon tree.*

Bones, twisted in agony, nowhere to go.
And his balls, rough and round and … *heavy.*
The end.

TY *picks up an old lemon and throws it at* NEDDY.

NEDDY *smiles.*

NEDDY: That's fucked.

NEDDY *picks up a few lemons and throws them back at* TY.

For a second—
Thought you had—
A—
Real—
Fuckin'—
Story!

They laugh.

TY *tries to dodge the lemons.*

TY *trips and lands on* NEDDY*'s machine.*

It's broken.

Pause.

TY: Fuck.
I'm sorry.
I'm really sorry.
I can—
Help you fix it.

NEDDY *is silent.*

We can make it even—
Even better—
Than before.
I promise.

Pause.

NEDDY: Doesn't matter.

TY: It does—

NEDDY: Just leave it.

TY: No—

NEDDY: LEAVE IT!

Not gonna work anyway.

Pause.

TY: It's not your fault, Neddy.

You were fighting—

NEDDY: I was fighting—

TY: You couldn't stop them.

NEDDY: Ten of 'em coming at me from different sides—

TY: Ten?

NEDDY: Well, a heap.

And I—

Pause.

If they'd just let me go—

I'd get her back.

TY: You will.

You know, you gotta take time with these things.

Whitefellas aren't like us.

Need to … watch them. Learn about them.

That's … what I reckon.

Pause.

Rivers dry up.

And stuff stays … dormant.

Like, asleep.

Baby fish. Plants. Bugs. Whatever.

And they sleep sleep sleep, just waiting for a drink.

And when it comes—

They know what to do.

NEDDY *looks at* TY.

TY *looks at* NEDDY.

NEDDY *leans in and stops.*

TY *does the same.*

They both want the same thing.

They kiss.

They kiss again.

They pull apart.

NEDDY: Yeah.
TY/NEDDY: Cool.

Pause.

TY: Again?
NEDDY: Again.

They kiss.

TY: Again?
NEDDY: Again.

They kiss.

TY/NEDDY: Again?

They kiss.

TY: Wait.
        Is this the—
        Like—
        Have you done this—
        Am I the first?

Pause.

NEDDY: Yeah.
        First for the day, anyway.

        NEDDY *and* TY *look at each other.*

    Have you grown?
TY: Don't reckon—
NEDDY: Like, in the last few minutes—
TY: Unlikely—
NEDDY: Nah—you're taller—

        NEDDY *pushes* TY *playfully against the tree.*

TY: I'm still the same, dickhead!

NEDDY: See! Couldn't rest your head on this branch before—

TY: Didn't *try* to—

NEDDY: Couldn't do—

This.

Before.

NEDDY *gently presses his body against* TY.

NEDDY *kisses* TY*'s neck.*

Pushing him against the tree, NEDDY *moves his body against* TY.

We see NEDDY*'s back, and* TY*'s face.*

Excited. Nervous. Unsure.

But mainly excited.

It feels good.

It feels even better.

It's over.

NEDDY *and* TY *slide down the tree.*

They're a bit astounded by what just happened.

Cool.

TY: Yeah.

NEDDY: Yeah.

There's some quiet.

They stay close.

TY: I was up all night, you know. Just me and the moon and the fire.

And my aunty came out and she said—

'Who ya achin' for, eh?'

You know—in that creepy 'I know fucking everything' aunty way—

And I told her about you.

But don't be freaked out—

It was just, like, a mention.

And she said—

'Better get yourself back to him.'

So I did.

Pause.

  I feel like …
     A grasshopper.
     Boing.
     Ah fuck.
     That's weird.
     I'm weird.
     I'm sorry.
NEDDY: I used to catch grasshoppers and stand on them.
     Make 'em crunch.

     Pause.

TY: Okay.

     Pause.

  This might sound—
     But what if we just never went back?
NEDDY: Where could we go?
TY: We could cut down this tree.
     And carve out like, a place to sit.
     And we could float down the river for ages.
NEDDY: The river goes past both our mobs—
TY: A chance to meet everyone?
     Say 'Hello!'
     'We're off for a float!'

     Pause.

  My aunties would *love* you.
NEDDY: You reckon?
TY: They'd ask you lots of questions and make you lift things.
     It's just what they do.
NEDDY: My mob would like you, too.
TY: Yeah?
NEDDY: My uncle would make you describe things. He loves that shit.
TY: Ummm—
NEDDY: Because you notice stuff—

Like, I bet when you look at … a puddle—you'd talk about …
all the different *blues*—like, kinds of blue—reflected from the sky
onto the water.

Or some shit.

And that's—

That's nice.

TY: You think so?

Pause.

NEDDY: Back to the log.

TY: Yes.

When we get somewhere nice, on the log, we could stop.

NEDDY: What's there?

TY: Everything is lush. You know? Like … *lush.*

NEDDY: And there's a waterfall?

TY: Yeah!

NEDDY: And a big flat rock that sits right in the sun—

TY: And we could lay there—

NEDDY: And bake like lizards—

TY: And do what we just did.

NEDDY: Yeah. And do that.

TY: A lot.

NEDDY: A fuck load.

TY: And every tree has something different growing on it, and there
are animals everywhere, and the birds wake us up in the morning—

NEDDY: But not too early.

TY: Nah, at a good time.

And we can go between the water and the rock and when it rains
there's a cave to hide in and—

Yeah.

NEDDY: Nice.

Silence.

We can do all that.

As soon as—

And it won't be long—

But—

As soon as I'm back.

Silence.

TY: The Elders told you to stay.

NEDDY: And?

TY: They know what's—

NEDDY: I'm not gonna sit around and wait—

TY: It's not *waiting*—

You need to watch and—

NEDDY: Watching hasn't done us any good so far, has it?

TY: Elders have reasons.

NEDDY: Like what?

TY: Not stuff you or I can know.

NEDDY: Well I know *exactly* what to do.

I'll go down over the hill.

They're still there. Whitefellas don't move around much.

Reckon she's there.

Somewhere.

TY: But if she—

If she *isn't*—

There, I mean—

NEDDY: What?

NEDDY *stands up.*

TY: Like, if she's … gone.

It's not—

It has nothing to do with—

It's not your fault.

NEDDY *is irritated.*

NEDDY: I know she's there.

TY: I know—

NEDDY: She's waiting and she knows I'm gonna come and she'll see me running over the hill—invisible to everyone 'cept for her—and she'll know that it's all gonna be … good.

TY: Yeah.

NEDDY: Yeah.

Pause.

Ty?

What if I didn't try hard enough.

TY: What do you mean?

Pause.

NEDDY: If I didn't—

Fight.

TY: Neddy—

NEDDY: If I hid instead—

If I watched her get taken away —

If it was my uncle who fought 'em off—

If—

If I cried behind a tree.

TY *holds* NEDDY *close.*

Then—

Distant sounds of dogs barking and whitefellas yelling.

NEDDY *pulls away from* TY *and listens intently.*

NEDDY *climbs the tree.*

He looks off into the distance.

TY: What is it?

NEDDY: Smoke.

Dogs.

If I can talk to 'em—

TY: Talk to them—?

NEDDY: If I can get to 'em—

TY: They'll kill you the moment you get anywhere near—

NEDDY: I'll raise up my hands.

I dunno.

Gotta try.

Don't I?

Pause.

TY: I'll come with you.

NEDDY: No—

TY: You'll need help—

And they live along the river, so I know about—

NEDDY: I've got it all figured out—

TY: Let me help—

NEDDY: You've got your own job to do back home—

TY: That can wait—

NEDDY: It's important.

> And they chose you.

> *Pause.*

I'm gonna go find her.
> And I'm gonna do it myself.

> *Pause.*

Learn the stories and save 'em up for when I'm back.
> I'll lay right there.
> And you'll lean up against the tree.
> And you can tell me everything you know.

> NEDDY *kisses* TY.

> NEDDY *runs off into the scrub—*

> *But—*

> *He suddenly turns back.*

> *He kisses* TY *again.*

> NEDDY *leaves.*

TY: Please come back please come back please come back.

> *The tree grows, taking more Country for itself.*

(D)

Next moon.

And the next moon.

And the next moon.

TY *waits.*

The first time, he's hopeful.

The second time, he's concerned.

The third time, dread.

TY: Neddy?

4.

A few months later.

A full moon.

Rotted lemons all over the ground.

TY *has fallen asleep under the tree.*

NEDDY *appears.*

He whispers to TY.

NEDDY: Hey.

Ty—

Ty—

TY *wakes, startled.*

TY: What—

Neddy?

NEDDY: You expectin' someone else?

TY: It's dark—

I—

Neddy—

Where have you—

How did you *get* here—?

NEDDY: It's been hard to get back—but I came as soon as I could—

TY: Did they catch you?

NEDDY: I have to wait till they're sleeping to do anything.

And this is the first time that—

So—

TY: I don't get it—

NEDDY: It's not easy to explain it all—

But I'm here.

Pause.

TY: They just ... let you go?

NEDDY: Well, no—

TY: You escaped?

NEDDY: No—

TY: I thought you were—
    I didn't know if I'd—
    Can I touch you?
    You're not a spirit?
    You're real?
NEDDY: Real as the dirt.
    And I've got so much to tell you—
TY: Me too—
NEDDY: I've missed you—
TY: I've missed you—
NEDDY: These whitefellas—I tell ya—
    They fucking stink.
    Like they never seen a river or heard of water.
    Wrapped up in clothes they been wearing since *birth*, basically.
    Open their mouths and it's like a waterfall of stink.
    Mosquitos who get too close drop dead.
    Rocks turn green.
    Sticks catch fire.
TY: Ewwww.
    So what happened?
    I've been imagining … everything.
    Literally everything.
    So what have they—
    What did they do to you?
    Did they hurt you?
NEDDY: It's not like that.
    The thing is—
    They get me to help them.
    You know?
    It's not like what we've seen.
    So I've been with them and watching them—
    Like you said—
    And learning about them—
    And they think I'm there to help.
    Pretty smart, eh?
    But get this—
    They said there's a camp—

Up north—
Where they've got girls—
Same age as Sis—
And I'm gonna get to go up there.
Soon.
They said *soon*.

Pause.

TY: So you're going back?
NEDDY: I have to—
TY: Came here just to say you're pissing off again—
NEDDY: But just for a bit—
TY: Have a good trip, then—
NEDDY: But I wanted to come back and see you—
TY: Uhuh—
NEDDY: Talk to you—
TY: Great—
NEDDY: Tell you the plan—
TY: Thanks for that—
NEDDY: Thought you might think it's—
Brave.

Pause.

Isn't that good?
TY: Sure, Neddy.
Exchange over.

TY *goes to leave.*

NEDDY: Wait wait wait wait—
Come on—
I'm back.

NEDDY *tries to be playful.*

Have you grown since I last saw you?
TY: It's been four fucking moons.
I've had time to grow and then shrink again with old fucking age.
Why didn't you come back?
Why didn't you try and tell me that you were … *helping them*?
That you've been … *fine*?

NEDDY: Not as simple as—

TY: Every day I heard something different. One day, someone's seen you dead at the foot of a tree, next day someone's seen your muddy footprints near a lake. Dead, alive, dead, alive.

And then your mob started sending someone else.

NEDDY: What'd they say?

TY: I can't tell you.

NEDDY: What?

TY: I can't tell you.

NEDDY: Come on—

TY: Not your job anymore.

You've got your hands full with—

Whatever the whitefellas tell you to do, obviously.

NEDDY: Just tell me what they're all sayin' about me—

TY: Not till you answer some questions—

NEDDY: I'll answer whatever you—

TY: Where have you been—how are you not dead—how are you not tied to a tree—how are you not hungry or thirsty or tired—how come you've got that fucking *bounce* still—how come you haven't asked me anything—how come you lied—how come you—

NEDDY: Okay okay okay okay okay okay okay.

I'll tell you.

Just—

Stop for a second.

Sit down.

TY *doesn't sit.*

Sit.

TY *stands a little taller and straighter.*

Fine.

I went there—

Well, before I went there, I got a branch.

Big dry one.

For their fire.

Enough for a whole night—

You shoulda seen—

TY: I get it.

NEDDY: Dragged it down the mountain.

Came at 'em slowly.

They didn't do anything. Just watched me.

And I left the branch and walked back to the edge of the bush and just waited for a while.

They just stared like dead fish—

They didn't realise the branch was—

TY: For them.

NEDDY: They got the idea later. Two blokes came out—

Took two of 'em to drag somethin' that I carried by myself—

TY: Yes, you're very strong.

NEDDY: So every day I took something different.

More wood and sometimes a dead roo or—

You know.

Just stuff.

And I just got closer and closer to the camp and—

And one day they let me in.

And now—

I've got this special spot to sleep.

On this mat.

And there's food.

Pause.

TY: And that's it?

NEDDY: And now I've got an idea of where Sis might be—

TY: I imagined you with your hands and feet tied up, with gashes all over your face, with cloth stuck in your mouth, with sticks and muck all through your hair and a hoarse voice from crying out 'no!' and 'help!' and maybe even my name—

NEDDY: Had to stay and build trust—

TY: I trusted you'd come back. Can't take trust from me—from *us*— and give it to a bunch of whitefellas—

NEDDY: I'm doing it for Sis—

TY: No-one's seen her, Neddy.

Not Coast Mob, not my mob—

Not since—

Not since.

NEDDY: Bullshit.

> They *told* me there's a whole camp of girls.
> That's where she is.
> And you can tell that to my mob.
> To whoever they've got comin'.

TY: They don't want to hear from you, Neddy.

> They said—
> They said you went against the Elders.
> So there's no place for you anymore.
> They said—
> That you're not to go back.

> *Pause.*

  I'm sorry.

NEDDY: Whatever.

> Because I'll find her.
> And they'll have to get down on their knees—
> Beg me to come back.

> *Pause.*

  Is he prettier than me?

TY: Who?

NEDDY: Whoever they're sending.

> *Pause.*

TY: He's fine.

NEDDY: What?

TY: He's nice-looking, I guess.

NEDDY: You're supposed to say—

> You're not supposed to say that—
> You think he's prettier than me?

TY: No—

NEDDY: Wait—

> Did you kiss him?

TY: No—

NEDDY: I've been away and you've been kissing messenger boys from all over—

> Probably kissin' boys who just *look* like they've got a message—

Anyone who stands still for too long—holding a stick—open their mouth to take a sneeze and you wiggle your little tongue in there—

Is that what you've been doing?

Because even though you think I've just been hanging out—

I don't want to be there—

I don't want to help them—

And I think about you all the time—

Like, all the time.

It's kind of annoying.

So yeah.

Pause.

TY: I don't like him as much as the other guy, anyway.

So don't worry.

NEDDY: I'm sorry what who is this other what did you just say—

TY: It's not too serious.

He drops by every now and then.

We share a lizard, though.

Take turns feeding it.

And I'm about to carve his name into my thigh.

That's because I can't reach my own arse.

NEDDY: Oh.

Oh.

Yeah.

Funny.

Pause.

So just to make sure—

TY: There's no-one else.

NEDDY: Okay.

That's—

That's real good.

Pause.

Shit.

I haven't asked you anything.

How've you—

TY: We found one of our mob in the river.

     They said it happened so quick.

     Little hole straight through his shoulder.

     Blood all through the river.

NEDDY: Gun.

TY: What?

NEDDY: The hole's from a gun.

TY: You know a lot now.

     Pause.

We're starting to run out of stuff to eat—

     And the Elders keep wanting us to move—

     Whitefellas get closer and we move—

     Move move move move—

     Had to leave our spot and now we're ages away from our sacred places—

     And I'm cramming everything into my head—

     'That bend in the river means'—

     Something.

     And I'll wait for a nod from the wind or the water or a leaf to fall down.

     But—

     There's nothing.

NEDDY: You've got to stay safe.

TY: Where's safe?

     Pause.

NEDDY: Can I touch you?

     TY *nods.*

     NEDDY *touches* TY*'s face.*

Your face is the same.

     And your hair is the same.

     Pause.

I'm sorry.

     Pause.

TY: I thought you were dead.

TY *clings to* NEDDY, *upset.*

NEDDY: I know—

TY: Just stay, okay?

    We can go up north ourselves—

    You and me—

    I'm faster than I used to be—

    Bit stronger, too.

    And then you can come back to my mob.

    Live near the river. Together.

    NEDDY *kisses* TY.

NEDDY: This is the last time.

    I promise.

    I'm going straight there to get Sis.

    Then I'll bring her back here.

    You'll get along.

    I reckon you would.

TY: But now that you know where she might be, why do you need to go?

NEDDY: Only way I'll get close is if I'm with them. If they think I'm on their side.

    I'll have to go soon.

    They like to know where I am—

TY: A bit longer won't matter—

NEDDY: It will—

    It does—

    If they think I'm off with—

TY: Me.

NEDDY: Anyone other than them.

    Pause.

  Ty?

    I am coming back.

    Just need a bit more time.

TY: How long?

NEDDY: Two moons.

    That's it.

TY: Yeah.

    It's not that long, I guess.

    Just hope you don't get caught up.

    Again.

    Pause.

    NEDDY *starts to hum a tune.*

    It's not very good or particularly discernible.

    He picks a spot and clears away some of the lemons.

  What are you doing?

NEDDY: The whitefellas have this—

TY: Don't want to hear about it—

NEDDY: It's a good thing.

    You've gotta stand here.

TY: I'm not doing anything you learned from them.

NEDDY: The light's just right.

    Okay.

    I want to be with you for ever and ever and ever.

    And you want that too—

TY: Do I—?

NEDDY: You do.

    So.

    We'll do a ceremony.

    And we'll be stuck together.

    It's like glue, but with words.

TY: Right.

NEDDY: Usually there are flowers, but we don't have those.

    And usually there are guests—

TY: But we don't have those.

NEDDY: But the main thing is us.

    The ceremony is about *us.*

TY: Just go back to the whitefellas and get it done, okay?

NEDDY: You're gonna love this.

    I promise.

    So, we need the costumes.

    Something special.

    For you—

NEDDY *pulls out a canvas tent from his bag.*

Wrap it round you.

TY: I look like an egg.

NEDDY: A very nice egg.

NEDDY *gives* TY *a fan.*

And this. It's for when it's hot.
And for me—
Ummm—
This.

NEDDY *empties out his bag and puts it on his head, like a top hat, but shit.*

TY: Now what?

NEDDY: Just trying to remember.
Oh yeah.
We stand here.
And there's a man standing between us.

TY: Doing what?

NEDDY: Talking. Standing very still. Looking a bit fat.
And he says 'today…'
In a deep voice.
'Tooooday—'
'We are here toooooodaaaaay—'
'Todaaaaaay is a daaaaaay—'

TY: Wow.

NEDDY: That's not even the good bit.
We stand under a cross.

NEDDY *quickly carves a cross into the tree.*

And we look at each other.
And the fat man says more stuff.
La la la la la—
Blah blah blah blah—
And now—
We say things.

TY: Like what?

NEDDY: About what we like and what we'll always do—

TY: Well—

NEDDY: I'll go first.

> Ty—
> Since we first met—
> Things have been different.
> But they've always been good.
> Until I went away.
> And then I missed you.
> Which was very painful.
> Like being hit with a stick—
> Not just once—
> Or even twice—
> But lots of times.

TY: Wow.

NEDDY: I promise I'll come back.

> And we'll find a log.

TY: Carve out a spot.

NEDDY: Maybe an extra one for Sis.

TY: I promise I'll be here when you get back.

> *Pause.*

Now what?

NEDDY: The fat man makes sure we know what we're doing.

> This is forever.
> We're gonna be tied up like worms wrestling in the dirt.

TY: Okay.

NEDDY: Joined like a stringy shit to a wombat's arsehole—

TY: Yuck—

NEDDY: Forever and ever and ever we'll be—

> Us.

TY: And now?

NEDDY: We kiss.

TY: Kiss?

NEDDY: Yeah.

> We do.

> TY *and* NEDDY *kiss.*

> *Like two people on their wedding day.*

TY: So that's it. Forever.
NEDDY: I think so.
>Until one of us dies.
>Or finds someone better.
TY: Fuck off.

>*Dawn approaches.*

>NEDDY *realizes he's stayed too long.*

NEDDY: Well.
>I should go.
>Before they notice I'm not there.
TY: Already?
NEDDY: It's a long way.

>NEDDY *kisses* TY.

Two moons, okay?

>TY *holds* NEDDY *close.*

>*The tree watches.*

>NEDDY *starts to leave.*

>TY *holds his arm, just for a moment.*

TY: New rule.
>Only excuse for being late is being dead.
NEDDY: What if one of us gets stuck in a ditch?
TY: Climb out.
NEDDY: Or our feet get chomped off by rats—
TY: Walk on your hands—
NEDDY: Or we get stuck doin' a big shit—
TY: Shut up.

>NEDDY *leaves.*

>*The dawn light is warm and promising.*

(E)

Next moon. And the next.
TY *waits at the yella tree.*
He's wearing the makeshift wedding dress.
Like a bride abandoned at the altar.
He's anxious.
Then—
After waiting for a while—
He's pissed off.
He takes off the dress, and chucks it away.
TY *tries to remember stories, the fragments tumbling out of him.*

TY: Fish can tell you things about the river—
  They can help you sing the rain—
  When it's dry—
  Have to sing to the fish so that you can sing down the rain—
  I can't I can't I can't I can't—
  The bends in the river are like a—
  Lie—
  Tell a lie and you'll find a—
  On the other side of the river—
  I can't I can't I can't I can't—
  I CAN'T.

5.

A lot of time has passed.
In whitefella time, it's been two years.
There's no fruit or flowers on the tree.
Just leaves like knives.
Rigid and more dangerous than before.
The boys aren't boys.

There's something different about both of them.

NEDDY *is wearing different clothes.*

Whitefella boots.

A whitefella jacket.

They are distinctly from the early period of invasion.

NEDDY*'s taking a piss against a tree.*

TY *appears, holding a spear.*

He thinks NEDDY *is a whitefella.*

TY *raises the spear—*

And then—

NEDDY *turns around.*

He screams.

NEDDY: Ty—?
> Fuck.
> You coulda said somethin'—

> *Pause.*

How are you?

TY: I'm waiting for someone.

NEDDY: What?

TY: Exchanges. Someone will be here soon.
> Not sure they're gonna want to see you.

NEDDY: From my mob?

> *Pause.*

TY: What are you wearing?

NEDDY: Just … clothes.

TY: Whitefella clothes.

> NEDDY *motions to the spear.*

NEDDY: You a warrior now?

TY: Elders gave it to me.
> Learning how to use it.

> *Pause.*

NEDDY: Brought you this.

NEDDY *offers some bread to* TY.

TY: Don't want it.

NEDDY: You're hungry.

TY: Used to it now.

NEDDY: Take it.

TY: No.

NEDDY: Come on—

TY: No.

NEDDY: Don't be like this—

TY: What do you want?

NEDDY: I don't want—

    I came back.

    Like I said.

TY: You said two moons.

    It's been two years.

NEDDY: I've been working—

    Trying to keep them away from you and your mob—

    From *all* the mobs—

TY: How's that going for you?

NEDDY: Everything I'm doing—

    Everything I'm learning—

    It's to help you—

    To help us.

TY: That jacket gonna help us?

    Those boots?

    I waited—

NEDDY: I tried—

TY: How hard?

NEDDY: I did—

TY: Probably too fat and woozy from eating meat all day long—

    Too sleepy by the fire to even notice the moon—

    To think about *me*—

NEDDY: I did … think about you.

    Telling me stories while I went off to sleep.

    Sleep is the hardest thing—

    But a bit easier when I can hear you in my head.

TY: Stories have done fuck all for me.

Pause.

So why are you back?

Found your sister?

NEDDY: No.

> Not yet.

> Still … looking.

TY: Up north?

NEDDY: Turns out that wasn't … right.

TY: Surprise.

NEDDY: Takes time.

> *Pause.*

How are you, Ty?

TY: I've gotta do an exchange, Neddy—

NEDDY: Who are they sending?

TY: Different people. Sometimes I don't hear from them for ages.

> Sometimes they turn up.

NEDDY: You heard anything about … about my Uncle?

TY: No.

> *Pause.*

NEDDY: Are you okay?

> *Pause.*

TY: It's been—

> Shit.

> Okay?

> Exchange over.

NEDDY: I'm sorry, Ty—

TY: Everyone got sick. All of my Elders.

> I've got dirt under my nails—dirt everywhere—from all the digging and burying and my eyes feel all scrunched up from the—the—the saying goodbye.

NEDDY: What did they look like?

TY: First, they went limp. Like, could barely walk.

> And then bumps came up everywhere—like ants crawling around under their skin.

NEDDY: No no no no no—

TY: And they cried out and the Old People told us to stay away—to leave them.

NEDDY: You've got to keep your distance—

TY: And we lit fires. Left some water, just within their reach.

NEDDY: Ty, you can't go back there—

> This thing—
> The bumps—
> It's getting mobs from all over—
> You catch it from each other.
> Don't bury them.
> Don't touch them.
> Okay?
> It's bad.
>
> *Pause.*

You've gotta come back with me.

TY: What?

NEDDY: Come back to the whitefellas.

TY: No.

NEDDY: You got a better idea?

> You need to go back to your mob—
> Don't get too close—
> And find any anyone who isn't sick—
> Bring them too.

TY: Nobody is gonna want to do that.

NEDDY: You'll die.

> Come back with me, and we can find a spot for you.
> You'll have to do some stuff.
> But you'll all be together.
> And I'll be there, too.
>
> *Pause.*

We have tents.

> Places to sleep.
> And mine could be near yours.
> So at night—if we listened *hard*—
> I could hear your breathing and you could hear mine.
> And in the mornings—

We'd have to get water.

So we could go together.

That could be our thing.

They trust me—so I get a say in stuff like that.

So every day we'd get to be close.

And at night they all drink and bullshit around the fire. And we could sit back in the shadows a bit. And watch.

TY: And the others?

NEDDY: We'll find jobs for them.

Tracking or looking after kids or something.

And we'll keep your mob together.

Whoever's left.

The Elders would want that, wouldn't they?

Pause.

TY: We can't sleep together?

NEDDY: No.

We can't do that.

But near—

TY: Yeah, near—

NEDDY: And maybe we could talk through the walls—

TY: Tell you stories—

NEDDY: Whispered—

TY *moves towards* NEDDY.

TY: And when it's dark and there's no moon, I can slip into your tent—

TY *touches* NEDDY, *who recoils slightly.*

And take off your stupid boots.

And your dumb jacket.

And then—

Do—

This—

Hands running everywhere.

TY *removes* NEDDY'*s jacket.*

NEDDY: It's cold—

TY: Not for long.

NEDDY *resists slightly. Not in a big way.* TY *probably doesn't even notice.*

TY *removes each of* NEDDY*'s boots.*

TY *gently guides* NEDDY *to the ground.*

There's kissing and rhythm and puffs of breath.

NEDDY *stares at the tree, looming over them.*

NEDDY: Can we not—
   Can we move over there?
TY: Huh?
NEDDY: Just wanna move over a bit.

TY *kisses* NEDDY *as they awkwardly move away from the gaze of the tree.*

TY *kisses the length of* NEDDY*'s torso.*

Heading down down down.

Then—

A big noise.

Like a branch falling.

   What was that?
      Who's there?

NEDDY *jumps up.*

TY: Just a branch or something—
NEDDY: Ssshhh.
   Get over there.
TY: Why?
NEDDY: If they see me with—
   If they see us, we're fucked.

NEDDY *quickly starts to put his clothes and boots back on.*

TY: There's no-one there.
NEDDY: Sir?
   That a whitefella out there?
   It's me.
   It's Ned.
   Just after firewood.

Silence.

TY: That how you talk to them?

NEDDY: Got to, don't I?

Pause.

TY: You know what.

I think—

I'm gonna go.

You do your own thing, Neddy.

I just—

I can't.

I can't go there and be *near* you but not *with* you.

NEDDY: They've got their own ways.

TY: Right—

NEDDY: They say that if you …

If you do what we do—

Lightning comes down.

Ground opens up.

TY: Bullshit.

NEDDY: Haven't seen it—

But they all talk about it.

TY: No-one's gonna die or explode from a kiss.

NEDDY: It's not the kiss—

It's the—

TY: You and I.

NEDDY: Ty—

You don't reckon anyone could see us?

Even from up in the sky?

TY: Good luck, Neddy.

TY *leaves.*

NEDDY *shouts after him.*

NEDDY: Come on!

Food that you don't gotta kill with your own hands.

And stuff to keep ya warm.

And you can sleep, like, *really* sleep—because you know they're not comin' to get ya in the dead of night.

And I just thought—
I just want to keep you safe.

Pause.

Fuck.

NEDDY *looks up at the tree.*

(F)

NEDDY*'s at the whitefella camp.*

TY *is by the river, obviously in pain.*

NEDDY: Those who do wrong will not inherit.
Those who do wrong will not inherit.
Forgive me because I have—
Forgive me.

TY: Fish can tell you things about the river—
They can help you sing the rain—
When it's dry—
Have to sing to the fish so that you can sing down the rain.
I CAN'T.

TY *looks to the sky.*

I'm sorry.
I'm trying to remember them all, Aunty—
But I don't know who's gonna be left to listen.
Aunty?

Pause.

Fuck you, Neddy.

TY *lifts up his shirt.*

Red blisters cover his torso.

It's smallpox.

TY *curls over in pain.*

But he pushes through it to tell a story.

There's a bird who sits in a tree.
And no-one ever sees the bird.

No-one watches the bird come or go.

No-one gives a fuck about him.

And every day something was lost.

And the bird wore those things—the memory of them—like a necklace of stones—

Weighed down and choking.

The sky was a stranger.

The bird could never take off.

Flashes of light.

TY *appears, covered in blood.*

NEDDY *appears.*

Neither know what to do.

6.

Under the yella tree.

Soon after.

TY *is unwell but trying to hide it.*

NEDDY: Shit shit shit shit shit shit SHIT SHIT SHIT SHIT SHIT.

TY: It's okay—

NEDDY: You killed whitefellas—

TY: Listen—

NEDDY: We're dead—

We're dead we're dead we're dead we're dead—

TY: Neddy—

NEDDY: They'll have thirty blokes out looking for you by morning. And there'll be money for whoever gets you. And they'll spit in your face and drag you through mud and near-on kill you for days and days and days because to kill you would be a kindness and that's not how they work.

TY: Neddy—

NEDDY: I don't wanna hear it—

TY: I'm—

NEDDY: Don't want to know why—

TY: I'm fucked, Neddy.

TY *lifts up his shirt.*

There are angry red spots all over.

NEDDY: What—?

TY: Yeah.

NEDDY: Oh fuck.

TY: Watched them for so long—
　　　Stayed *away* for so long—
　　　And they still got me.
　　　Felt good to do something—
　　　To finally—

NEDDY *drops to his knees in prayer.*

NEDDY:　Guide us waking—
　　　And guard us sleeping—
　　　Almighty and merciful—
　　　Bless us—
　　　And keep us—
　　　Please.

TY: Stop it.

NEDDY: Ask him to be gentle.

TY: *Who?*

NEDDY: Ask him to have mercy.
　　　He'll listen—

TY: No—

NEDDY: Do it.

TY: Don't want your whitefella bullshit—

NEDDY: That's why this is happening—

TY: There's no mercy in whitefellas.
　　　None.

NEDDY: Ty—

TY: Don't want to hear it—

NEDDY: My turn for once.

Two spirits came to visit a man. And he took them home. And they took off their clothes. And he lay with them, like a man should lay with a woman.

And he suffered.

Within himself.

And then—
Flashes of white light.
And his body—
Turned against him.

Pause.

TY: Better ending:
They … press their palms into his back—
NEDDY: They didn't—
TY: They smile.
There's no flash of white light.
No punishment coming down.
The spirits slip away.
And there's quiet.

Pause.

We did the whitefella ceremony.
NEDDY: And I got it wrong.
We *can't*.
Forget that.

NEDDY *paces.*

Why didn't you just come back with me?
All of this could have been… better.
TY: They're all gone now.
All my Elders.
And I'm the only one who knows the stories.
And who am I gonna tell them to now?
Tried whispering them to Country.
But the dirt is sick.
Poisoned.
NEDDY: I'll take care of you—
TY: How?
You pull away if I get too close.
You shiver like it's cold when I touch you.
How're you going to take care of me?

Pause.

NEDDY: We asked for this.

TY: Asked for it?

NEDDY: Think about it.

      When we started—

TY: Started what?

NEDDY: You know what I mean—

TY: Just want you to say it.

      Just want you to give it a name.

      Whisper it if you want.

      So the whitefellas don't hear you.

NEDDY: We started—

      And then my sister went.

      And now you're sick.

      It's the cost.

TY: Everything around you seems to die.

      Me. Her.

      Grass on either side of your boots.

      Just like them, aren't you?

NEDDY: Just a different—

TY: Don't you remember?

NEDDY: No—

TY: Your body, my body, close together, feeling good—

NEDDY: Stop it.

TY: Feeling *good*—

NEDDY: STOP!

TY: Got your belly full and your feet covered up with fuck knows what.

NEDDY: That's not true—

TY: Where's your sister then?

NEDDY: Stop—

TY: Stopped looking?

NEDDY: Shut up—

TY: Forgot what her face looks like?

      Forgot her voice?

NEDDY: They said she might have been moved—

TY: They seem to say a lot of stuff—

NEDDY: They said—

TY: Words words words words—

      Whitefella words.

Pause.

She's *gone.*

Silence.

Come on—
  You've known for a while.
NEDDY: I looked.
TY: Neddy—
NEDDY: This whole time—
    I—
    Really looked.
TY: To start with.
    But now?
NEDDY: Shut up.
TY: You're there for the food and the warm and the fancy coats.
NEDDY: Shut up!
TY: You didn't fight—you didn't try to save her—you cried behind a
  bush while she got dragged away and you just watched—
    But look at you now—
NEDDY: SHUT UP!

    NEDDY *can't look at* TY.

I'm gonna forget everything.
    Your eyes and your voice.
    And—
    In a while from now—
    I won't know your name.
    Even if I hear it.
TY: At least you'll have the sky to talk to.
    Hope he answers back—

    Silence.

    NEDDY *and* TY *are both upset.*

NEDDY: Ty?
TY: Thought I'd feel better.
    Thought it might clear my head.

    Pause.

Just wish I listened more.

I've got bits of knowledge and stories and I try to scrape around in my brain for anything I can remember.

NEDDY: You know it.

TY: It's got to be more than that though—I've got to be it. To walk it and sing it and speak it and remember all the places that take a lifetime to know and remember.

To do what the Elders asked me to do—

To do a good job.

NEDDY: They knew they could trust you.

A disturbance close by—dogs barking.

Shit.

TY: Just go.

Leave me here.

NEDDY: No—

TY: I'm not good, Neddy.

NEDDY: I can't—

TY: Take off your jacket.

NEDDY: Ty—

TY: Listen.

Take off your jacket.

NEDDY: Take off my jacket?

TY: And your boots.

NEDDY: And boots—

TY: Cut your hand open.

NEDDY: Cut my hand—

TY: And rub blood all over it.

NEDDY: Rub my blood—

TY: You got it?

NEDDY: I think so.

TY: Chuck them by a river bank and run as quick as you can.

NEDDY: Run as—

TY: Quick as you can.

Remember how fast you are?

NEDDY: What are you going to do?

TY: I'll stay here.

I'll wait.
And soon enough—
I'll be with everyone again.
My Aunty.
The whole mob.
So don't worry about me.
NEDDY: Ty.

NEDDY's upset.

We were gonna float down the river—
TY: Neddy—
NEDDY: Past both mobs—
Sit in the sun—
TY: I know—
NEDDY: Fuck all day—
And just be together.
TY: We messed it up.

Pause.

You need to go.
But—
Come back—
And take me home? Some day?
Whatever's left.
Find me a spot near the river.
Put me in the ground.
Somewhere I can hear the water.
NEDDY: What about your mob—
TY: There won't be anyone.
Promise?

Pause.

NEDDY: Promise.
I should've come back.
I should have known that she was—
TY: Go.
NEDDY: Ty—
TY: GO.

NEDDY: I—
TY: I know.
NEDDY: If—
TY: I know.

> NEDDY *can't say goodbye.*

> *The sounds of the whitefellas getting closer.*

Go!
NEDDY: No—this way!

> NEDDY *drags* TY *to a spot where they can huddle and hide.*

> NEDDY *holds him close.*

> *Darkness.*

7.

TY *and* NEDDY *huddle under the stars.*

TY *is unwell, fading in and out.*

NEDDY *desperately tries to comfort him.*

TY: The stars are there.
> Aunty says—
> Keep track—
> Watch them—
> But don't blink—
> Or you'll miss one.
> Count them.
> One.
> Two.
> Three.
> Four.

> *Pause.*

> TY *drifts away.*

NEDDY: Please come back please come back please come back.

> NEDDY *tries to remember something.*

There was a spirit—
> Who lived by the river.

There was a spirit who lived by the river—right at the crossing where you could leap from rock to rock and get across safely.

She was beautiful.

And the men who came across her fainted at the sight of her slender arms and her breasts.

And she'd …

TY: Drag them—

NEDDY: Drag these men into the river, where she'd leave them to rest for ever and ever, catching glimpses of her figure as she stretched out on the river bank.

One day a beautiful young man came along, hoping to cross.

And he looked her in the eye.

And he asked for safe passage.

He didn't faint at the sight of her.

The spirit was angry.

'My beauty brings men to their knees!'

The man replied—

'Your beauty is undeniable.'

'But—my heart sings for—'

Someone else.

He points across the river to another young man, waiting patiently.

In a rage, the spirit soaked the dirt around the river, and mud pooled at their feet.

'You can—'

Pause.

TY: They can stare.

NEDDY: At each other.

Until—

Forever.

And they did.

They never felt warm breath on their cheek.

They wasted away, their ankles locked in the filth.

They became …

Stone.

TY: No—

They stretched out their arms—

And they became trees—

NEDDY: Growing growing growing across the river—
TY: Waiting until they could finally—
NEDDY: Finally—
TY: Touch.

> *The tree becomes more and more unstable.*
>
> *It falls.*
>
> TY *and* NEDDY *reach for each other—*
>
> *And then—*
>
> *Blackout.*

THE END

www.ingramcontent.com/pod-product-compliance
Lightning Source LLC
Chambersburg PA
CBHW050020090426
42734CB00021B/3357